MY FUNNY VALENTINE

Jokes and Riddles

for Kids Ages 8-12

This Book Belongs to:

_____

_____

THANKS!

Thank you for your purchase. If you en-
joyed this book, please consider drop-
ping us a review by scanning the QR
code. It takes only 5 seconds and helps
small independent publishers like ours.

Scripto Love
PRESS

Contents

Introduction

Add a little joy this Valentine's Day with *My Funny Valentine Jokes and Riddles for Kids*! Jam-packed with festive jokes, riddles, and puns about all things Valentine's Day, it's sure to deliver hours of "hearty" laughs for the whole family.

Whether you're reading alone, or with others, these laugh-out-loud jokes are sweeter than a box of chocolates!

1
Animal
Valentine's
Jokes

Why didn't the two dogs make serious Valentine's Day plans?

It was only puppy love.

What do you call two birds in love?

"Tweethearts!"

Do skunks celebrate Valentine's Day?

Yes, they're very scent-imental!.

What Valentine's message can you find in a honeycomb?

"Bee mine."

What do girl snakes write at the bottom of their letters?

"With love and hisses."

What do owls say to declare their love?

"Owl be yours!"

What do you write in a slug's Valentine's Day card?

Be my Valen-slime.

What do you say to an octopus on Valentine's Day?

I want to hold your hand, hand, hand, hand, hand, hand, hand, hand!

Why was the rabbit happy?

Because somebunny loved him.

Knock, knock!

Who's there?

Luke.

Luke who?

Luke who got me a valentine!

What did the one sheep say to the other?

"I love ewe!"

And how did the other sheep respond?

"You're not so baaaaaa-d yourself!"

What did one cat say to the other cat on Valentine's Day?

"You're purr-fect!"

**What did one bee
say to the other?**

"I love bee-ing with
you, honey!"

**What did one squirrel say
to the other squirrel on
Valentine's Day?**

"I'm nuts about you!"

**When do bed bugs
fall in love?**

In the spring.

What did the girl squirrel say back to the boy squirrel on Valentine's Day?

"You're *nuts* so bad yourself!"

Which animal shares the most love?

A heartvaark.

What did the sheep say to the other on February 14th?

"Wool you be my valentine?"

Knock, knock!

Who's there?

Olive.

Olive who?

Olive you with all my heart!

**What did the whale say
to his sweetheart on
Valentine's Day?**

"Whale you be mine?"

**What do you get when
you kiss a dragon on
Valentine's Day?**

Third degree burns
on your lips!

**What do bunnies do when
they get married?**

Go on a bunnymoon!

**How did boy bat and girl
bat spend Valentine's Day?**

Just hanging around.

**How do werewolves
send Valentines?**

By hair-mail!

**What did the buck say to
the doe on Valentine's Day?**

"You're a dear."

**What are insects called
when they're dating?**

Lovebugs.

**What do you get when
you cross a dog with a
valentine card?**

"I love you drool-ly."

**Why did the rooster cross
the road?**

He wanted to impress
the chicks!

What did the boy elephant say to the girl elephant on Valentine's Day?

"I love you a ton!"

Did you hear about the nearsighted porcupine?

He fell in love with a pin cushion.

What did the boy bear say to the girl bear on Valentine's Day?

"I wuv you beary much!"

Knock, knock!

Who's there?

Atlas.

Atlas who?

Atlas, it's Valentine's Day!

What was the French cat's favorite Valentine's Day dessert?

Chocolate mousse.

What did one bee say to the other?

"I love bee-ing with you, honey!"

Why did the horse miss the Valentine's Day Dance?

He had hay fever.

2
Food
Valentine's
Jokes

**What did the tomato say
to his girlfriend on
Valentine's Day?**

I love you from my head
tomatoes!

**What did one piece of
toast say to the other?**

"You're my butter half!"

**What kind of candy is
never on time?**

Choco-LATE.

What did the chef give to his wife on Valentine's Day?

A hug and a quiche.

What did the strawberry say to his valentine?

"I love you berry much!"

What did the dry grape say to his wife?

You're the raisin I smile.

Why did the Melon go out with Berries?

Because he couldn't get a date.

What did the cucumber say to his friend?

"You mean a great dill to me."

Why did the boy put candy under his pillow?

"Because he wanted sweet dreams!"

Knock, knock!

Who's there?

Butter.

Butter who?

Butter pucker up Valentine!

What did one watermelon say to the other on Valentine's Day?

"You're one in a melon!"

What do Italians say to each other on Valentine's Day?

"You've got a pizza my heart."

Why are we like chips and avocados?

"You guac my world!"

What did one pickle say to the other on Valentine's Day?

"You pickle my funny bone."

Where do all the hamburgers take their girlfriends on Valentine's Day?

To the meatball.

What did the cook say to his girlfriend?

"You're bacon me crazy."

**What did one mushroom
say to the other on
Valentine's Day?**

"There's so mushroom in my
heart for you!"

**What did the baker say to
his sweetheart?**

"I'm dough-nuts about you!"

**What happens when
you fall in love with a
French chef?**

You get buttered up.

Why did everybody want to be Miss Banana's valentine?

Because she is very a-peeling.

What did the chocolate syrup say to the ice cream?

"I'm sweet on you."

What food is crazy about Valentine's Day chocolates?

A cocoa-nut.

Knock, knock!

Who's there?

Bea.

Bea who?

Would you Bea my Valentine?

**What did the apple say to
his wife on Valentine's Day?**

"I love you sweetie pie!"

**What Valentine's Day candy
is best to give a girl?**

Her-She Kisses.

**What's the perfect thing
to say to a coffee-lover on
Valentine's Day?**

"Words cannot espresso what
you mean to me."

Knock, knock!

Who's there?

Al.

Al who?

Al be your Valentine if you'll be mine.

3
Love
Valentine's
Jokes

**What did the stamp
say to the envelope on
Valentine's Day??**

"I'm stuck on you!"

**What did one light bulb
say to the other on
Valentine's Day?**

"I wuv you watts and watts."

**Why did the sheriff lock up
her girlfriend?**

She stole his heart.

**What did the painter say
to her sweetheart?**

"I love you with all my art!"

**Why is Valentine's Day a
good day for a party?**

Because you can really
party hearty.

**What do you call a ghost's
true love?**

Their ghoul-friend.

How did the doorbell propose to his girlfriend?

He gave her a ring.

What did one volcano say to the other?

"I lava you!"

What do you call the world's smallest Valentine's Day card?

A valen-tiny.

Knock, knock!

Who's there?

Sherwood.

Sherwood who?

Sherwood like to be your Valentine!

**What the most popular
shape on Valentine's Day?**

An acute triangle.

**Have you got a date for
Valentine's Day?**

Yeah, it's February 14th.

**What did Frankenstein's
monster say to his bride on
Valentine's Day?**

"Be my Valen-stein!"

What flowers get the most kisses on Valentine's Day?

Tulips (two-lips).

Who always has a date on Valentine's Day?

A calendar.

Why don't you ever date a tennis player?

Because love means nothing to them.

What did one oar say to another?

"Can I interest you in a little row-mance?"

What did one flame say to the other on Valentine's Day?

"We're a perfect match!"

What did the drum say to the other drum on Valentine's Day?

"My heart beats for you."

Knock, knock!

Who's there?

Disguise.

Disguise who?

Disguise is your boy friend!!

**What did the ghost say
to his wife on
Valentine's Day?**

"You look so BOOtiful."

**What did the tree say to
the houseplant?**

"Do you beleaf in love?"

**What did the calculator
say to the pencil on
Valentine's Day?**

"You can always count
on me."

What did the refrigerator say to the magnet?

"I find you very attractive."

What did the scientist say to his sweetheart?

"We've got great chemistry!"

What did the stamp say to the envelope on Valentine's Day?

"I'm stuck on you!"

What did one Jedi say to the other on Valentine's Day?

"Yoda one for me!"

What did the dustpan say to the broom?

"You sweep me off my feet!"

What did cavemen give their wives on Valentine's Day?

Lots of ughs and kisses.

What is the difference between a girl who is sick of her boyfriend and a sailor who falls into the ocean?

One is bored over a man, and the other is a man overboard.

Did you hear about the man who promised his girlfriend a diamond for Valentine's Day?

He took her to a baseball park.

What's the most romantic ship?

A courtship.

Knock, knock!

Who's there?

Pauline.

Pauline who?

I think I'm Pauline in love with you.

What was the thunder cloud's favorite gift to give on Valentine's Day?

A Box of Shocklates.

What did the pencil say to the sheet of paper?

"I've had my "I's" on you since childhood."

Why is loving you like an old pair of dentures?

Because I can't smile without you!

**Did Adam and Eve
have a date?**

No, they had an Apple.

**What did the shoe
say to the lace on
Valentine's Day?**

"You're my SOLE-mate."

**What did one piece of
string say to the other?**

"Be my Valen-twine."

**What's the most romantic
city in England?**

Loverpool.

**What did the guy
with the broken leg
say to his nurse?**

"I've got a crutch on you!"

**I once fell in love
with someone who
only knew 4 vowels?**

They didn't know I existed.

Knock, knock!

Who's there?

Heywood.

Heywood who?

Heywood you be my Valentine?

Why did the skeleton break up with her boyfriend before Valentine's Day?

Her heart wasn't in it.

What kind of flowers should you not give on Valentine's Day?

Cauliflowers!

What do farmers give for Valentine's Day?

Hogs and kisses.

What do you call someone with a cold on Valentine's Day?

Lovesick.

How does cupid deliver Valentine's all over the world?

On an arrow-plane.

What two words have a thousand letters in them on Valentine's Day?

Post Office

What did Pilgrims give each other on Valentine's Day?

Mayflowers.

What did one font say to the other on Valentine's Day?

You're just my type.

What happened when the two angels got married?

They lived harpily ever after.

Knock, knock!

Who's there?

Pooch.

Pooch who?

Pooch your arms around me.

What does a carpet salesman give his wife for Valentine's Day?

Rugs and kisses.

What did the fisherman say when he proposed to his girlfriend?

"You are o-fish-ally my favorite person."

What did the cat write in the Valentine's Day card?

"I love you meow and forever."

4
Valentine's Puns

**Muffin can ever come
between us.**

Olive you.

I wheel-ly like you!

I love you s'more and
s'more each day.

Orange you glad I'm yours?

I turtle-y love you.

You make my heart pop!

Here's my number,
so kale me, maybe?

You give my life porpoise.

I've got my ion you!

I love you so much and that's all rhino!

I only have fries for you.

You're sud-sational!

Made in the USA
Monee, IL
10 February 2023

27458628R00037